UNCOMMON SENSE RETIREMENT

UNCOMMON SENSE RETIREMENT

Because Common Sense Doesn't Seem Very Common Anymore

Mark Henry

For information contact:
Phone: 1-800-689-3935
Fax: 1-877-496-9797
Email: info@veritasretirement.com

ISBN Hardcover: 978-1-939758-52-1
ISBN eBook: 978-1-939758-53-8

Library of Congress Control Number: 2014902759

Cover design by Natspearldesign

Dedication

*To my beautiful wife, Terri,
without whom this book would never have been written.
Having her love, friendship, support, and unwavering
faith allows me to reach further
than I ever would have thought possible.*

*To my children, Hunter, Amy, and Seth,
I thank God every day for blessing us with you.*

*And to my close friend, Pastor Chris,
who tries so hard to keep me from crashing
into the guardrails of life, but who always
accepts me when I still occasionally bump into them.*

CONTENTS

PART I

The Times They Are A-Changin'

CHAPTER 1

Uncommon Sense for Retirement: Joe Is No Longer Enough

WHEN IT COMES to financial planning and, more specifically, planning for the golden years of your retirement, what should you take into account? Diversifying your portfolio? Leaving enough money for your children? Avoiding certain tax traps? These are all key elements to consider while articulating long-term goals for retirement.

But there's an unspoken irony to traditional retirement planning, too. I've seen hundreds of hard-working folks make the same mistake. They spend years planning to retire, yet they forget to plan for the most important part: sustaining themselves to the finish line.

The typical understanding of retirement planning only gets a person so far. Which is why I feel that within the current typical model of financial planning, we must begin to understand the landscape with uncommon sense. I call it "uncommon" simply because common sense isn't very common anymore! Financial planners seem to have forgotten it, and as a result, they make things far more complex than they have to be. In this book, I'm embracing *uncommon* sense, in the hopes that I can put common sense back where it belongs: at the center of your plan for a happy, healthy retirement.

Let's first take a look at who exactly is falling into retirement pitfalls these days, which, unfortunately, is the majority of retirees and pre-retirees. Most of the clients I serve are generally fifty and older, and have a net worth ranging from $100,000 to over $2 million.

Most of these people have already saved and saved well. What they're missing is a core concept that they may not have been aware of: Saving to this particular point is only half the battle. Having enough to see out the golden years of retirement and leave a lasting *legacy* is the true goal.

The common saver within this financial bracket already has an advisor. These savers often use "big box" financial management companies, which specialize in helping them put away enough money for the day they stop working. The first unfortunate drawback is that customers at this level rarely get the same personal service as the clients who earned upwards of ten times their net worth. The second drawback is that financial management companies do an excellent job helping their clients get to the first phase of retirement, but there is another phase, so often forgotten, that demands adequate preparation. For you to plan in terms of legacy and "after the finish line," a more all-encompassing personal strategy needs to be put in place.

My goal in this book is not to teach you how to *save* for retirement. There are plenty of books, videos, and seminars chock-full of ways for you to save and invest your hard-earned income—for me to walk this well-trod path would be repetitive and just about worthless. What *I* believe is that I can guide you into taking a different look at financial planning as a whole—to shift your focus and strategy in a way that helps you execute a multipronged approach to give you the greatest return on investment for all the time and resources you've put in. The saving has already been done. Now what do you do with it?

Hank and Joe

The following case study could be any of my clients—it's a situation I've seen all too often. Hank is fifty-five years old and has a net worth just shy of $1 million. He should certainly have enough for a comfortable retirement, right? But as a result of traditional retirement planning, Hank has a large percentage—more than 90 percent—of his wealth in high-risk investments. His risk tolerance has always been pretty high, and as long as he is in the accumulation phase, that's okay. But as he moves closer to retirement with the majority of his funds still at risk, he is putting *himself* at risk, too. A sudden market drop could drastically change things for Hank. Today he is perfectly comfortable, but he's one market reality away from a very different story.

Hank's financial manager, Joe, has done an incredible job of getting Hank to this level of savings. Unfortunately, Joe works for a large financial management and investing company. He answers to many higher-ups who have wants and demands that have nothing to do with his client Hank. Further complicating the problem is the fact that Joe also serves a wide range of similar clients. Joe essentially lacks the ability to help Hank move forward past the saving phase—and now Hank needs practical tools for utilizing the hard-earned money he's made.

In an ideal world, saving a large sum of money would be the end of the long road. From the outside, everything looks rosy: Hank has saved nearly $1 million and has earmarked portions of that money for his church, his favorite charities, and his only child, Rachel. But keep in mind: Hank doesn't want to simply leave a large 401(k) to his daughter, as it could create a potential large tax issue.

Rachel, in particular, stands to suffer from this old-school approach. When her father passes, what if the sudden windfall of inheritance pushes her into the next tax bracket? At that point the sum of her inheritance will rapidly deplete, solely from the higher taxes she is forced to pay.

Joe has been able to get Hank this far, but he lacks the abilities to make this money work for Hank all the way to the end. I'm not saying it's Joe's fault, nor is it the fault of his company. What is at fault is the generally misguided way most of us look at retirement saving. Frankly, before Hank even thinks about parceling off his savings, he should focus on the stability of his saved income. Hank is still alive and kicking—he still has to live on his retirement savings. Ironically, some of the steps he took to set aside this nest egg can now become detrimental to him actually keeping it.

On the road to accruing his savings, Hank has been advised to handle his money in certain ways that conveniently sidestep the current landscape of American tax policy. But inevitably—as with gas prices and the fluctuating economy—changes will occur that not even the sharpest investing managers are able to foresee. Hank needs the help of someone who can provide him with a strategy that yields a tax-free income stream that is *consistent* and that meets his ongoing needs.

Your Retirement

One of the first questions I ask when taking on a new client is: "What does retirement look like for *you*?" I want to see their vision for retirement—income goals, the lifestyle they picture, and the legacy they hope to leave. I want to take the time to really *see* my clients and help them live their best life. Another unfortunate drawback to the machine that Joe is a part of is that he just doesn't have the time, and sometimes the means, to provide tailored, personalized service to each and every one of his clients—even if he wants to. *Especially* when they cross over into the distribution phase.

Most of the clients of Joe's company are not able to afford that particular type of treatment unless their net worth falls into the category of $10 million and upwards. My goal is to provide double-digit millionaire service to the clients who are working with far less than that, and who aren't receiving that level of service now. Not only do they deserve that treatment, but they also need it the most. The retiree with $10 million doesn't have to worry as much about whether or not his money continues to work for him. Someone like Hank, on the other hand, must painfully deliberate the destination of every last dollar.

As I've mentioned before, many of the challenges faced by Hank and others in his predicament stem from the problematic equation "savings = the end." It's an outdated way of viewing retirement planning. Retiring in today's world is different than it was fifty, thirty, or even ten years ago. Things have changed.

Someone may have taught Hank how to *grow* his 401(k), but did anyone teach him how to distribute it and even pass it on? The bookends of birth and death are not the only constraint the average citizen has to worry about. What if Hank wants to develop a multi-generational IRA that continues down his familial line? The old ways work just fine if the end goal is to achieve a fixed benchmark of savings. But when it comes to leaving a legacy, they just won't cut it.

I've mentioned a few tangible ideas about preparing for the mysterious second half of retirement savings—but like so many important things in our lives, there isn't one answer, one magic bullet to fix it all.

Retirement investment should be looked at as a wheel with equally helpful and important spokes—each with a different and unique strategy but working in tandem to push the wheel forward. These spokes can be many things: a tax reduction strategy, a Social Security analyzer, a flexible strategy that can handle unforeseeable events well, diversification (through different types of retirement accounts rather than just different stocks). Ideally, each wheel will be uniquely designed.

Take, for example, the married couple who recently sat in my office. I asked the husband about his goals for retirement, and he informed me that he loved his job and that he planned on working until he was seventy years old. I then asked his wife when she saw herself exiting the workforce. She had a more calculated answer: 287 days, eight hours, and thirty-two minutes. She had even factored in vacation days so that she could get out as soon as possible!

I use this story to illustrate that even a loving couple who are planning their future together may still require unique plans for each person. I firmly believe that *your* retirement will not be the same as *their* retirement, or anyone else's for that matter. I also firmly believe that God gave us two ears and one mouth for a reason: I strive to listen twice as much as I speak.

Groundhog Day and the iPod Nano

A strong relationship with one's financial advisor is just one more aspect of retirement planning that has fallen by the wayside, thanks to the antiquated model of retirement planning. Because of the mainstream way of looking at retirement planning, most people aren't even aware that there are other options, other phases, and other equally important facets. Much like the protagonist in the film *Groundhog Day*, the amateur investment planner is stuck in a continuous loop—repeating the same mistakes, day after day, year after year, decade into decade. Bill Murray's character learned that nothing would change if he kept repeating himself; we must take a page from his book and learn the same lesson.

Most of us throw our good sense out the window because we've been conditioned to think about the retirement challenge in one particular way. We continue to exercise the standard practices, day in and day out, without making much overall progress. There are better ways right in front of us, if only we use uncommon sense. But we've been hypnotized into this rut, into a repetition of imperfect practices. The simple solutions exist—we just have to snap out of our current way of thinking, like Bill Murray when *Groundhog Day* finally came to a close.

Here is how I explain this concept during my

seminars: First, I hold up an iPod Nano. Now, that may seem like a pretty well-known piece of modern technology. But due to the age and priorities of my audience, some people have never seen this particular product. Nor do they see the dots along the timeline that brought the Nano from its origins to where it is today.

I explain to them how it works. "This small, sleek device can hold thousands of songs," I say. "It runs on a very small battery so that you can have nearly your entire music library accessible at the touch of a button, anywhere you desire. You can listen to your songs while running along the beach!" We laugh over the fact that before this technology was developed, you'd have to have a hulking boom box with eight massive batteries or run a wildly long extension cord from who knows where.

The people at my seminars who have never seen an iPod Nano are generally delighted. I explain to them how this little device has changed the way I listen to music—and it can change the way they listen to music, too. The fact that they've never heard of it doesn't negate how cool it is, how useful it is, how pleasurable it is.

That's my service. I am the iPod Nano. Some people may be stuck in the boom-box version of retirement planning because they simply know no other way. But that doesn't mean another way doesn't exist, that another way isn't cooler, more helpful, and more pleasurable. They just need to be made aware of it—and break free of their *Groundhog Day* cycle.

That is my vision. I want to show people that there is another way, another option, one that picks up where Joe leaves off. There's a step after him. And, more importantly, that step doesn't require six different people handling six different things. I want to show them the whole picture, with $10 million-dollar-client service for clients with a fifth of that net worth. I want to take them to the finish line, or at very least give them enough solid information that when they're done with me, they can get themselves there. I'm so very passionate about this that I work as hard helping my clients plan for their retirement as I do planning my own!

Some people get so worried about their money, they end up never spending it. I strive for a retirement that allows me to leave a legacy rather than just leaving money, one that affords me "sleepability"—because if you're going to bed worried and losing sleep, then you probably haven't done something right when it comes to your retirement.

At the end of the day, my goal is simple: I want to make a change in the way you see your retirement picture. I want to help change your future for the better. And if I can't do that, I at least want to leave you with the following kernel of wisdom: Joe is no longer enough.

By the time you've finished reading this book, you'll be armed with a boatload of wisdom and tangible actions to get you where you want to be. If I've done my job, you'll feel informed and empowered, ready to make your last years your best years.

CHAPTER 2

Coming Down the Mountain

WE'VE LOOKED AT the trappings of what we *think* is retirement planning—and seen how they will only get you so far. And we've seen how people like Joe can be very well equipped to get you through the first phase, or the accumulation phase . . . but maybe not the second.

In other words: You're going to have to come down the mountain. And if you plan well now, it's going to be a much smoother ride than if you don't.

In this chapter, I want to show you ways to solve the unique challenges of retirement in a more *uncommon sense* way. It's nothing new or revolutionary. Remember: Uncommon sense is just common sense that no one is using anymore! It's merely a process of putting simple tools and strategies in place to protect, preserve, and increase your retirement income and reduce your tax obligations along the way.

Retirement planning has two phases. The first is the accumulation phase—the money you save and put away during your working years. The second is the distribution phase: your golden years of retirement. For me, those phases correspond with two parts of the biggest climb of your life. Climbing the mountain is the accumulation phase. Going down the other side is the distribution.

Like everything worth anything, planning for retirement involves challenges. I like to look at these challenges like a mountain climber preparing to climb Mount Everest. Is it going to be difficult? Probably. But it's doable—if you make the right preparations for both the ascent *and* the descent. The wise mountain climber not only prepares to reach his goal—ascending to the peak—but also factors in the journey back down the mountain.

Retirement planning is much the same. Most financial advisors are well equipped to help you during the accumulation phase, but the moment you retire and cease to create income in the ways you have been creating income for decades, it all changes. What *I'm* trying to do is prepare you for the other side of the mountain. During the distribution stage, the goal is to use your preparation as a toolbox, utilizing your financial tools and savings to enjoy the remainder of your life.

Far too many people planning their retirement—and the financial advisors they enlist along the way—have been led to believe that to retire well they must focus simply on getting to the top of that mountain. They view the accumulation stage and the distribution stage as one long, steady climb. In reality, you are preparing yourself for two extremely different yet equally important journeys. There are two finish lines.

The first happens as you get close to retirement.

The second is the long—and rich, and wondrous—descent down the mighty mountain.

This second race, this "coming back down the mountain," is precisely where my specialization comes into play. I want to help you make what you've achieved in the first leg of the journey work for you through the second. To do that, however, I have to get you to think about your retirement differently.

When I say I want to impart uncommon sense strategies for your retirement, I'm talking about the same common sense that prevents you from putting your hand in fire, from touching an exposed wire, or from walking out into traffic—the obvious conclusions for your optimal well-being.

And yet, traditional retirement planning has been slow to get the memo. For many years, people and organizations have positioned the true "goal" as the moment you reach the top of the mountain. The consequence? We've altered our perception so that we now look at the journey through a skewed lens—without the clarity of common sense. We've tricked ourselves into making it more complicated than it has to be!

My goal in these pages is to make it simple again.

Safety and Risk

As we get older, shouldn't we be more cautious with our finances? The answer seems abundantly obvious. Ask yourself the question: "Do you agree that in our later years, we must be safer with our money?" If you're like the men and women who attend my seminars, then your answer is a resounding "Yes." That's pure and simple common sense right there. But what do we mean when we say "safer"?

The things you did at age thirty-five or forty, when you were still *making* money, may not be appropriate when you're sixty or seventy. The younger a person is in this journey, the greater their ability to take more risks as they have the opportunity to save for many years to come. When you're edging closer to your golden years, however—the top of the mountain—you simply can't afford the same amount of risk.

When I ask someone if they would rather be

wealthy *or* know that they won't ever run out of money, the overwhelming response is "I want to know I won't ever run out of money." Wouldn't you agree?

I was doing a seminar when the tsunami hit Japan. It was literally happening while I was up there speaking—people were reading the news on their iPhones and Blackberries. There were people in the room who were worried about how the tsunami would affect their retirement accounts. They had serious concerns about what might happen to their investments the next morning, and they shared those concerns with the group.

I felt terrible for those people, and not for the reason you might think. I felt like the focus was totally wrong. We should have been concerned about the people in Japan, and what was going to happen to *them* tomorrow morning, not how it was going to affect our retirement dollars. Of course, I also felt bad for the people in that room. If our retirement dollars are that much at risk, maybe we've done something wrong.

When a natural disaster happens, does it affect markets worldwide? Overwhelmingly, the answer is yes. But our concerns were misplaced that day. Our focus was tragically off target. If the people in my seminar were protecting and safeguarding their retirement dollars the right way, they never should have been at risk.

One of my clients came to me at eighty-two years old and still had 94 percent of his retirement accounts at risk. Why? Because that's what he had done for all those years. He didn't know any other way—no one had told him there *was* another way. But what if the market drops 20 percent tomorrow? What if, instead of a tsunami in Japan, there's an earthquake in California, wreaking havoc on the U.S. (and international) stock market? It's quite likely that that drop would negatively impact his ability to maintain his lifestyle and stay on top of his expenses.

I think about the stress that one of those market drops would have on him. At eighty-two, does he really want that kind of stress in his life? Sure,

if his investments go down, eventually they'll probably come back up. But this man is eighty-two years
old—how long is he going to wait? Does he have
enough time for the market to rebound, just to get
back to where he was? Can he afford to wait for his
investments to get back to even?

This is why I'm so passionate about what I do.
Unforeseen events can have a drastic impact and
devastate a retiree. I want to make sure it never gets
there.

A Tale of Two Brothers

Here's a story I love to tell—for me it's a terrify-
ing but ultimately very helpful lesson in how things
can turn out if you're not adequately prepared.

Two brothers retire at age sixty-five. The first
one retires in 1962 with $1 million. The second
one retires in 1965, also with $1 million. They both
spend $50,000 a year of the money they put away
for retirement—an even 5 percent. Most people
would say it's a little high, but that's okay. I'm not
going to give them a hard time.

Brother #1, the one who retired in 1962, dies late in life and leaves a wealthy estate to his children. Brother #2 dies in his eighties, broke and living on Medicaid and Social Security.

What's the difference between the two brothers? They both spent the same amount of money in retirement. They were both in the S&P 500, nice blue-chip stock. And yet one of them died and left a nice estate to his children, while the other died penniless and alone.

What went wrong for Brother #2?

The answer is deceptively simple. The only difference was when they retired.

The three years between 1962 and 1965 changed everything. The early sixties were really strong. Brother #1 saw his money do great things for him between 1962 and 1965. Unfortunately, 1966 and 1967 weren't so good, but this didn't affect Brother #1, who was enjoying nice returns from the three years prior. Brother #2, unfortunately, was doomed from the get-go.

Once they got to the 1970s, the market went

down even more. Both brothers were still taking out $50,000 a year—but those three little years made all the difference. One brother died a millionaire, the other a pauper.

It's called market timing, or the sequence of returns. The day those brothers retired determined everything about how their lives would turn out. What control did Brother #2 have over that? Not a bit. He couldn't help when he turned sixty-five. And you want to know the craziest thing?

You can't, either.

We have virtually no control over when things happen. The market conditions may change, or we may be forced to retire sooner than we thought. These things are simply out of our control most of the time.

So what if you reverse it? If you put the losses at the beginning and the gains at the end? If you take it over the same thirty-year period, the returns would be exactly the same. If you add up all the pluses and minuses divided by the number of years you're calculating, you get the exact same average. But that doesn't take into account market timing. With the sequence of returns, everything changes. All of a sudden, somebody can go from cruising along comfortably to being completely broke. Remember: We're not adding money, we're withdrawing money, and we may have suffered market losses at the same time. And what control does a person have over market timing? None. You don't have any control over market timing. You don't know when the next loss or gain is coming.

All those things don't matter when you're still going to work. When you're in the accumulation phase, you may sustain losses, but you're still putting money in. When you get your check every month, money goes straight to that 401(k), buying you more shares. Each month you actually own more of the company. You keep putting money in and eventually it goes back up. And you love it because there's more of it!

When you're in the distribution phase, you experience the exact opposite. It's a double whammy. You're now retired and you've got to pay $50,000 to sustain your standard of living. You're used to making nice money. So you start making withdrawals —at $50,000 a year, let's say—and then experience a modest 10 percent loss. How much did your account go down? Try $150,000 in the first year of retirement! Let this happen a few years in a row and it doesn't matter how much you had to begin with— you'll never catch back up.

Everything backfires when you're no longer contributing. That's why the accumulation phase and the distribution phase are so different. It's like apples and oranges. A market loss during the accumulation phase simply means that, the next month, your money buys *more shares* because the cost of those investments went down. Let's say I put in $100 and it buys ten shares of Apple. If Apple goes down to $5 a share the next month, my $100 now buys *twenty* shares of Apple. That's the same $100, though now I get twice as many shares! Now if Apple goes back to $10 a share ten years from now, I own more shares; therefore I make more money. That's why dollar cost averaging works so well in regular investing. As long as you're contributing, everything's great.

Now let's apply the same logic to your retirement accounts. While you're still in the accumulation phase, if you're putting in $500 a month and your investments go down the next month, all it means is that you've bought more of each of those particular investments. Now, when the market comes back up, you own more shares, so your funds grow even more. That's just simple dollar cost averaging.

The flip side, however, is that a market loss during the distribution phase means you took money out, *and you also lost money.* Talk about being completely unprotected as you come back down the mountain! Like a hiker on Everest without a pack, without climbing gear—without even pants and a jacket.

In other words: It won't end well.

There is no one tried-and-true way to come back down the mountain. There are different tools in the toolbox, and I suggest a different combination for each client. A client with $2 million can afford certain risks in the post-retirement phase that a client with $50,000 cannot.

What is the money you're accumulated for retirement? It's nothing but *financial security.* Real security comes from someplace else. How much more of your financial security are you, right now, this year, willing to lose? There is no bad answer here. Some people tell me, "You know, I could stand to lose 10 percent and still be okay." For others, that number is less. In some couples, each partner has a different answer, and I work closely with them to bring their retirement expectations into alignment.

Risk isn't necessarily bad if you're willing to take it. As we move into the retirement phase, however, risk *must* be reduced. No matter what your risk tolerance was while you were growing your income, now it must be greatly, greatly reduced. I can't stress that enough. Otherwise, you stand far too great a risk of having something happen during the distribution phase that could drastically change everything.

Now that we know we must protect ourselves during this distribution phase, what does that really mean? Other than simply avoiding risks, how do we sustain ourselves in a period that seems to consist only of depletion? And, assuming we spent our accumulative years socking money away into the appropriate accounts and investment vehicles, how do we know which money to spend and which money to save?

When a Dollar Doesn't Equal a Dollar

Most people have two types of accounts for retirement: qualified and non-qualified. Your 401(k)s, IRAs, TSBs, 403s—all the alphabet soup—are called qualified accounts. This is money that you have not yet paid income taxes on.

Then we have the non-qualified accounts: money that you put away to save it. This includes your brokerage accounts, CDs, cash, maybe even a Roth IRA. This money is considered after tax—you don't owe any income tax on it, except maybe on the capital gains it has made.

Non-Qualified Accounts	Qualified Accounts
CD	IRA
CASH	401(k)
SAVINGS	403
Brokerage Account	TSB

Once you're in retirement, you're not working, you've got your Social Security and pensions coming in . . . and you need more money. So where do you take it from? Your IRA or your non-qualified other accounts?

Good question. Let's do a little exercise.

For this example, we're going to assume a Coca-Cola is still $1. And it's a Coca-Cola we've got to have. So we go to our non-qualified accounts, take out some money, and buy the Coke with $1. Pretty easy, right?

Now let's see what happens if we take $1 from our IRA account instead. Wait a second! We're in a 25 percent tax bracket. When we take $1 out, 25 cents has to go to our partner in those accounts: Uncle Sam. Now we have 75 cents. And 75 cents won't buy the Coke. If we want to buy that Coke, we have to take *$1.33* out of the IRA, pay 33 cents out in taxes, and now we have our dollar to buy the same Coke.

In both cases we got a Coke; but in one case we took $1.33 out and in the other we took $1 out. So which one should we use?

"Easy!" you say. "I don't want to pay taxes any more than I have to. I'll just use my non-qualified account." That makes sense, doesn't it? But there are some other things to factor in here. First off: Do you think taxes are going to go up or down? There are three things I personally believe are going to happen in our country no matter what:

1. Taxes are going up.
2. Government benefits are going down.
3. Inflation's going to happen.

If I were a betting man, I'd bet money on it. I know these things are going to happen—I just can't tell you which day.

So if taxes are going to go up, my 25 percent tax bracket may be 30 percent in the future. And inflation is definitely going to happen—that Coke will be $1.50 before long. I may have to pay more taxes later on. So maybe it makes sense to take the dollar out of the qualified account first, saving those other accounts for later so that when I DO make a withdrawal, I get 100 percent of what I take out.

Every case is different; there is no "right answer" here. All I'm encouraging you to do is open your eyes and think about this for a second, before we go and start taking out money.

And let me ask you another question, while I'm at it. What's your plan for that IRA?

The Crystal Ball

Financial advisors would be the hottest commodity on the planet if somehow we had access to a crystal ball. Unfortunately, I don't have one. It's important for me to get that across. No magic bullets, no perfect way to come down the mountain, and no crystal ball.

Why do people get into the stock market? To make money! If anybody ever tells me they're in it for emotional or sentimental reasons, I'll tell those people they are crazy. They're in it to make money. And how do you make money in the stock market? Buy low and sell high.

What do you need in order to do that? A crystal ball! And I don't have one. You've got to know, for sure, when a stock's low and when it's high, so you can buy it low and sell it high. And it ain't happening for most people.

While we're working, we put our money in the stock market because we know that we will accumulate money *over time*. That right there gives the game away: When you're eighty years old, that may not be the right plan for you. A winning strategy in the stock market must always be about time, and your time is drastically reduced when you're sixty, seventy, eighty years old.

As we said, we can predict certain things, like the fact that taxes and inflation will continue to go up. What *can't* we predict? The stock market. What happens when the market crashes? It wasn't too long ago, in 2008, that the market corrected with a huge setback. Say you lost 30 or 40 percent in the market that year. How long are you going to wait to just get back to where you were?

Time to go back to our mantra: What does common sense say? Unless you have a crystal ball yourself, you may need to look at a much more common sense approach to handling these precious retirement dollars. Let's reduce your risk and set up a clear plan with a goal in mind. Where are you going to take money from first? What are you going to leave and what are you not going to leave? Let's make this journey down the mountain a predictable one, and as warm and sunny as we can.

Do storms come at the right time in your life? Never in *my* life. It seems like the bad things don't happen at the proper time. You've heard that bad things come in threes, and as crazy as that sounds, it seems to be true in my life. You get thunderstorms and a tsunami on the same day. The key is to be as prepared as we can, so that we can emerge from the storms and sail smoothly back into the open sea.

PART II

Debunking the Seven Former Truths About Retirement

After more than thirty years of working in business and finance, I've heard hundreds of stories of well-intentioned men and women holding on to certain beliefs about their money. This is particularly true on the subject of retirement, where people cling to "former truths." I won't call them "myths," because many really were true at some point in the past. But these truths are no longer true now, and unfortunately, no one has bothered to update the old model. As long as people continue to believe them, these former truths are ticking time bombs waiting to explode.

I've seen so many retirees watch their retirement dreams change or completely vanish due to unforeseen changes in the market. All the while, these former truths are allowed to move about silent and deadly, perpetuated by some people who know better and some who don't. They move swiftly, spreading their poison among retirees far and wide, and if they remain unchecked, they can cause serious damage to investment portfolios and put retirees in compromising situations in regard to their financial health.

I want you to think of these former truths as a virus, and this section as a kind of vaccine. My company is named Veritas Retirement for a reason. Veritas is the Latin word for truth. In this chapter, I'm going to describe seven of the most common "former truths" I hear from retirees—and I'm going to give you the truth as I see it.

CHAPTER 3

FORMER TRUTH #1:
My expenses will go down when I retire.

TRUTH: Thirty or thirty-five years ago, this was true. People retired in their homes, and they weren't facing the longevity we enjoy now. Your grandfather's expenses probably did go down when he retired. But today this is no longer true. Your expenses are going to go up after you retire—no question about it.

AT THE END of the day, our ultimate well-being is dictated by our income—whether it be while we're accruing it or afterward, when we're depending on our savings *as* income. The clients who come to me tend to operate under the following false assumption: "When I stop working, I won't spend as much."

To be blunt: This idea is outrageous. It simply doesn't hold up.

First, let me say I understand how the misconception came to be. You get so trained in the lifestyle of working, you assume a very large chunk of your unwanted expenses are tied to the act of making money. How many expenses will you be relieved of once you retire? The answer is many. But the average retiree believes that these burdens will be lifted when, in actuality, the burden is only *shifted*.

Susan, one of my clients, recently rejoiced in explaining to me how much less she'd be spending during her post-retirement years. "I won't be paying to dry-clean my work outfits anymore!" she said. Susan's right about that. "I'll save money on all the gas I won't be burning from my daily commute!" Right again. But when these expenses disappear, others quickly appear to fill their place.

I asked Susan if she had any hobbies or activities she'd like to pursue through retirement. She did, of course—most of us do. She expressed to me that she hoped to spend more time playing tennis. With all the golden free time that retirement allows, she would have a surplus of time to play.

And yet. The luxury of more time to play tennis brings its own minor expenses, just like the ones that come with a daily job. Susan will pay for gas to travel to and from playing tennis, and she'll eventually purchase new fitness apparel, maybe even new equipment, to keep up with the hobby. And what if she wants to travel to play tennis at a relaxing vacation resort? Suddenly the expenses add up.

I'm not saying one shouldn't pursue these leisurely activities. In fact, quite the opposite: This is what retirement is for. But don't be fooled into thinking your golden years will be significantly cheaper than your working years. Even if you're not going on lavish cruises every other month, you're going to spend more than you think.

Your Retirement Income

Once you retire, where does your income come from? For most people, Social Security is one reliable, steady source of income. Married couples are able to depend on each partner's Social Security, which means two sources of income. Some people might also have a pension, or maybe even a few small pensions.

Add that up, and that's your retirement income. That's it. That's the money that will come in regularly each month. And if you've planned, if you've worked hard, if you're lucky, then maybe that's a good amount of income, and it affords you the lifestyle you want—until something happens.

What can happen?

Here's an example. A couple goes into retirement, and they each have Social Security. The husband also has a pension. The wife had the harder job—she stayed home with the kids—but it's the husband who has the pension. This income works for them. But when the husband passes away, his pension goes away, too. A lot of pensions are set up that way. So now, the wife has to take the higher of the two Social Securities accounts, and give up the pension. All of a sudden, she's lost one Social

Security and one pension. I assure you, that budget is not working anymore.

Even if the pension is set up differently, so that it doesn't go away, but is just cut in half, this woman is still down to one Social Security account and half a pension. All of a sudden, without warning, her income goes down, and there's not enough left for her to live anywhere near how she used to live.

The income offered by Social Security and a pension does not add up to the lifestyle that most people hope to live. To help supplement that income and to get the lifestyle they want, people will start to withdraw from their retirement accounts—the money they've saved over the years.

This is where income planning becomes crucial, because even people who have saved diligently, even people who draw only a modest 4 or 5 percent from savings each year, can wind up running out of money. This happens all too often. Market conditions change, investments aren't moved to safety, unforeseen things happen, and suddenly the money runs out. People get to the end of life and realize there simply isn't enough money. They've outlived their savings, and now they're in trouble.

So how can you get an income that's impossible to outlive? How can you take your Social Security payments and pension, and then supplement them with an income stream that you can't outlive?

This is one of the most overlooked parts of retirement planning . . . but not anymore.

Fixed Index Annuities

One of the most common ways of ensuring a lifetime income is through what's called a fixed index annuity (FIA) with a lifetime income benefit rider. This is essentially an insurance policy you can buy that will guarantee you a steady amount of monthly income for the rest of your life. When you move a portion of your IRA over to a fixed index annuity, it's still an IRA, so this counts as a rollover. Then you let it grow with the market, without the risk of losing the money. The income you draw is based on an accounting value, and while the money is in the account, it grows at a rate that could be as high as 6 or 6.5 percent per year.

Whenever you decide you need income, you turn it on, and the FIA becomes a source of regular monthly income that's guaranteed for as long as you live—even if the annuity runs out of money. When you want to take a withdrawal, you take one. When you don't need the income, you don't take it. So you draw from the annuity without losing control of your retirement assets.

Here's a real example: Chip is fifty-five. He's got a savings account, a pension he'll get at sixty-five, and Social Security, which he also plans to take at sixty-five. Chip would like to retire around sixty-two. And, like all of us, he doesn't want to run out of money.

So, he takes $100,000 out of his IRA and rolls it over into a fixed index annuity. He does this now, at age fifty-five, and he leaves the money there. At age sixty-two, seven years later, Chip decides to start taking income. He wants to be paid every single month. Over those seven years, he's taken his $100,000 and grown it in the annuity, so that now it has an income account value substantially higher than it was when Chip started. Based on that account value, he's going to get a guaranteed income paid monthly for the rest of his life.

Let's look at some simple math here: Chip is sixty-two when he turns on the account and lives to be eighty-eight. For the remaining twenty-six years of his life, he is paid back more than double what he initially put in. If Chip lives longer—let's say he gets lucky and lives to be 103—he's still guaranteed that payment every single month. If he changes his mind and he's happy working until he's sixty-five, that's fine, too. The money stays in the annuity and it means that when he does start taking an income, he'll be able to take more per month. Or maybe circumstances change and he needs to retire at sixty. He's still getting a guaranteed income for life. It's flexible, and he can control it. And no matter what he chooses, he has greatly reduced his risk, because he's moved a portion of his money into safety with the annuity.

That's one of the advantages of a fixed index annuity: You can put your money in and get a contractually guaranteed income for the rest of your life, basically a pension, that's not contingent upon market ups and downs. You've created a source of income that you cannot outlive.

Is this a perfect scenario? Is it something everyone should do? Is it a magic pill? No. But it's a useful tool that might be right for you.

CHAPTER 4

FORMER TRUTH #2:
I'm healthy, so I won't need
long-term care insurance.

TRUTH: Want to know your real risk of needing long-term care? It's either zero—you're never going to need it—or 100 percent! There is no in-between. It's kind of like winning a lottery: You either win or you don't.

A RECENT SURVEY estimated that, by 2020, twelve million older Americans will need long-term care. People who reach sixty-five will have a *greater than 40 percent chance* of entering a nursing home. That's more than four out of ten. You can look at a thousand people and say, "Maybe I'll be one of the four hundred, or maybe I'll be one of the six hundred."

But if you end up being one of the four hundred who do need long-term care, it's an overwhelming burden of expense. Why would you want to gamble against those odds?

Let's do a quick exercise.

I want you to grab pen and paper, and on the left side of the paper, I want you to draw a small square with a triangle over it. This is your first house.

Right next to it, draw another house. Then another one next to that. You should have three houses on your paper. Draw a **1** in the roof of the first house, a **2** in the second, and a **3** in the third.

In the box of the first house, write: **$250,000.**

In the box of the second house, write: **$25,000.**

In the box of the third house, write: **$200,000.**

Still with me? Good.

Now, below the first box, write **1/333.**

Below the second box, write: **1/8.**

And below the third box, write: **2/5.**

When you're done, your paper should look like this.

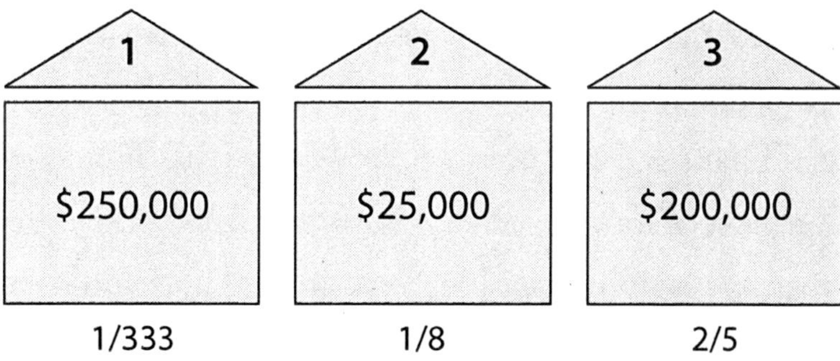

Now I'm going to tell you what those numbers mean.

House #1 represents the insurance on your house. The odds of you having a major claim are 1 in 333. I'm not talking about a few nicks on the paint—I'm talking, your house burns down or the roof gets blown off. The odds are 1 in 333 that this will happen to you. If you're like most people, your house is the most expensive asset you own, and it's worth insuring.

House #2 represents the insurance on your car. You're required by law to have liability coverage, but I'm betting you've got comprehensive and collision, too. The odds of you having a pretty good-sized claim are 1 in 8.

So what does **House #3** represent?

It's the odds of you needing long-term care in your life.

That's right: 2 out of 5, or 4 out of 10. The average cost of long-term care is around $200,000—and the cost is going up. Just look around and you'll see why. People are living longer and longer, which means people are ailing like never before. When I was a kid, we didn't know what "dementia" was. Today, the World Health Organization estimates 35.6 million people live with dementia worldwide. That number is expected to double by 2030 and more than triple by 2050.

We don't know where it's coming from. Is it cell phones? Diet Coke? The end result is the same: Long-term care is a huge drain on families. And virtually *no one* has done enough to prepare.

Now, I'm not telling you go to out today and buy long-term insurance. All I'm telling you is that the odds say we need to be prepared. I led you through the above exercise to show you how unbalanced it is, that we go to great lengths to prepare for disaster and damage to our "things"—our houses and cars— but not the most important thing: ourselves.

The 800-Pound Gorilla

At my seminars, I often ask attendees: "How many of you said on the way over, 'Man, I just can't wait to get to the nursing home?' But one in two of you are going! So why don't we talk about it? Is that common sense? No!"

And yet, it's the 800-pound gorilla in the room. No one wants to talk about it. I'm trying to get you to at least *think* about it.

You don't have to have a lot of money. A competent advisor can help you put together a plan so you can qualify for Medicaid if you ever need to. If you're healthy and still young, you can seek out a long-term care specialist. There are great long-term care options. They're still affordable when you're healthy and young.

What if you're not? What if you're like me and you're a Type-1 diabetic? Long-term care insurance might be priced out of the market for me, but that doesn't mean I shouldn't be thinking about it. And it doesn't mean I don't have options.

Remember the fixed index annuity we discussed in the last chapter? There are versions of the FIA on the market that come with a rider that says, if you can't perform two out of six activities of daily living, then the policy will pay out double for five years. If you're like me and you can't get long-term care insurance or the cost is prohibitive, then get that rider! You turn your IRA into a FIA so it provides guaranteed income for life, and then, if your health takes a turn for the worse and you can't perform two out of six activities, you can exercise the rider and begin collecting double. You may not qualify for long-term care insurance, but thanks to the rider, you'll have a new source of income to help cover your medical expenses and get you the care you need. And at the end of those five years, even though the income goes back to its original amount, it is still guaranteed at that level for the rest of your life. This is just one example. This product is out there and it can help some people who have the foresight to use it. If you don't qualify for long-term care, then you need to find different ways to provide for the care you'll need. If you have a lot of money, great—maybe that's a suitable solution.

Put a portion of that money away and plan for the worst. With luck, you'll never have to use it. But if you *do* end up needing long-term care, you'll use the portion of your money you set aside.

The key is: Everybody needs to have a plan for an event with these kinds of odds. You've got to be prepared for the worst. And if no one's ever talked to you about long-term care insurance before . . . then why in Sam Hill isn't your current advisor talking to you about something that's got a 2 in 5 chance of happening? Ask yourself that!

CHAPTER 5

FORMER TRUTH #3:
I'm going to pass my IRA off to my children.

TRUTH: The tax burdens your children are likely to incur can greatly change the amount of that gift.

I HEAR THIS one all the time. "I'm going to leave my IRA with $350,000 to my son. I'm going to leave my IRA with $500,000 to my daughter." That's great. It's a testament to a parent's love and generosity for their children that they want to leave them money.

Here's the problem: Unless it's given in the proper vehicle, you may not be giving them the amount of money you think you're giving them.

Money isn't free. It comes with future tax burdens

and a whole bunch of other headaches your child will have to face, when they're already struggling with the grief of losing you. With money, there are always strings attached.

Once you take into account the tax burdens and penalties, how much are you really leaving your kids? The answer is: probably not much. The key is to have a plan for a judicious, penalty-free way to leave an inheritance for your children—*without* all the strings attached.

The Stretch IRA

Either by planning or by accident, a lot of people bequeath money through their IRA. Ninety percent of all IRAs are cashed in—liquidated—upon the death of the second spouse. So, husband Tom has an IRA, he passes away, and his wife, Betty, takes over the IRA. She takes her minimal required withdrawals, and a few years later, she, too, passes on. Now what happens? Ninety percent of the time, the IRA is liquidated, emptied. The balloon is popped—all the air comes out.

What happens then?

Let's say our couple passes away, and their only son, Tom Junior, is forty-five years old. Before they died, his parents made him promise he would cash in their IRA when they were gone, so he could finally build that dream house for his wife and kids. That IRA was worth $500,000. What a score! So he liquidates their IRA and adds it to his current year's earnings. Now he pays taxes on his earnings *plus* the $500,000 his parents gave him, plus any local or state taxes that may be applicable at that time.

What kind of tax bracket is Tom going to be in when you give him $500,000?

Not a low one, I promise you that.

Did you know the highest tax bracket we've ever had in this country was 91 percent? Ninety-one! And that's not even an anomaly: There was an eighteen-year period in the United States where the tax bracket was consistently over 80 percent. For every dollar an American citizen made above a certain number, 80 percent went to the federal government. In this same sense, for every dollar taken out for a Coke, the government would get 80 cents!

Fast forward to now. We're on a twenty-four-year run of some of the lowest tax brackets this country has seen. Turn your uncommon sense on for a second: Do you think taxes are going up or down? We've had them as high as 91 percent, and we're currently on a twenty-four-year run where they're low. They're going up, my friend. Who knows what taxes might be when we give money to our kids? Taxes could go up to 60 or even 70 percent. How much money did you really give Junior? Not very much!

Enter the stretch IRA.

Tom is forty-five years old. Everything in the equation is the same, except for one little difference: His parents invested their money in a stretch IRA instead of a Roth or traditional. So when Tom and Betty pass on, there is $500,000 in their stretch IRA.

Tom Junior will take a small required minimum distribution (RMD) based on his age, starting this year. Let's assume that Tom Junior is going to live for another forty years, and that we can get that

IRA to generate 6 to 8 percent. If Tom continues to take out just his minimum required distribution, he is only paying taxes on this small RMD each year while the bulk of the IRA is still growing in value.

Then, he's going to turn around and leave the bulk of this inherited IRA to one of his children. So he leaves it to his daughter, who is thirty years old, and she starts doing the same thing. We're talking about making a legacy out of that money! Less than 10 percent of people are doing this, because most of them are cashing it in. But if they knew this option was available to them, I think they'd be singing a very different tune.

People don't know how to do this, and they're not setting up the accounts to do it, anyway. No one has helped them put the right structures in place. But I just gave you one of the best retirement strategies available—we're talking about changing lives here—and it's one you've probably never heard of.

There are a lot of ways to leave money to someone: You can write it in your will. You can put it in a trust. You can leave it in a CD and bequeath the CD when you pass away. What you want is a clear, thoughtful way of looking at things. A different way of looking at things. An *uncommon sense* way of looking at things.

Life Insurance

Here's another smart way to pass money to your children. Let's say you have $250,000 to leave to three children. You're pretty healthy, and you're pretty sure you're not going to need this money. What if you purchased a life insurance policy, and paid for it up front with that $250,000? Depending on your age and your health, that might get you $500,000, $750,000, or maybe even $1 million in coverage. Now, you've taken the money you wanted to leave to your children and you've doubled, tripled, or quadrupled it. *Now* when you pass away, they are going to get a much larger amount. And how are they going to get it? Tax-free. Life insurance isn't taxed.

If your own circumstances change and suddenly you need the money that you've invested in that life insurance policy—maybe you wind up needing to go into a nursing home and didn't expect to—some policies have riders that allow you either to take money out of the growth of that life insurance policy or access the funds of that big policy. When you're in the nursing home and it pays you accelerated death benefits, you can get some of the money sooner, to help you pay for your care. So you get great flexibility while still giving money to someone else. It's a really good tool.

What's the right way for you to leave money behind? There is no single right answer. There are a lot of great tools out there, and each of them is suited to different needs. You've got to see a specialist to find out what's the appropriate course of action for you. But the key is to look at what you want, and then be smart and creative with the tools that are available to you.

CHAPTER 6

FORMER TRUTH #4:
I've got enough retirement income because I live modestly.

TRUTH: Modest living is not going to protect you from rising healthcare costs and inflation. It simply won't. A gallon of gas is no longer 89 cents and the price of a gallon of milk continues to go up. It's not a factor of how modestly you live—it's a factor of how the world around you is changing.

"But Mark!" you say. "I've got my Social Security and pension! Trust me: I've got enough income to get by on."

Let me ask you this: Have you factored in how expensive things can get?

I don't want to scare anybody. I'm not trying to

exaggerate things or make you fearful of the future. But let's get our heads out of the sand and use some common sense about some of the challenges you might face.

In case you haven't noticed, we're not in fine form in the United States of America—at least not money-wise. We have overwhelming debt, we've got an unbelievable amount of people not working, we've got a heavy burden on Social Security, and we've got disability and Medicaid issues that are underfunded by enormous amounts of money. Whether or not you agree that our country is broken, it's certainly broke.

None of that is your fault. But unfortunately, it *will* affect you and your future as a retiree. What changes are going to have to happen to get our country back on track? And how will these changes affect you? I don't claim to have all the answers, but I do think it's foolish to assume everything will remain the same during your (and my) retirement years. It's simply not using common sense.

Believe me, I'll be facing the same challenges when I retire. I can tell you this right now: My retirement age may be ten years later than my dad's. Maybe even fifteen. I may be seventy-five before I can retire—we just don't know. I might get fifty cents on the dollar for what I'm supposed to get! Are there going to be changes? Yes! We don't even know how the new healthcare legislation is going to affect things. What is it going to cost in twenty years when I need to pay for my prescription medications? I don't want to think about it.

I recently met with the children of Barbara, a seventy-five-year-old retiree. Barbara's kids were looking for some answers for their mom, who tragically lost over 60 percent of her wealth in 2008. What did Barbara do after the markets crashed? Well, afraid to lose any more money, she took it all out and put it into a savings account.

Unfortunately, the tragedy just kept going. If Barbara had left her investments alone, those accounts would have come back up—at least some of the way. But her money has spent the last five years sitting in a savings account, earning virtually no interest. Between 2008 and 2013, had the retirement accounts been left in the markets, she would have experienced extremely large growth. Maybe she could have gotten most or all of her money back. Of course, you can't blame her for being too scared to take that gamble.

Now she's faced with going into an advanced care facility and *does not have enough money left*. This is someone who was set up financially very well. But a series of events changed her situation completely. And now she is so far into this heartbreaking chain of events, there's not a lot anybody can do to help her.

Can you blame a seventy-five-year-old who's lost 60 percent of her money for wanting to move it all into a savings account? She didn't know the market was going to go back up. She also didn't know she was going to have to move into an advanced care facility. Nor did she know she was going to fall into the doughnut hole—otherwise known as the coverage gap—and have to pay $500 a month in prescriptions.

This woman had enough money. What she *didn't* have was a plan.

For me, the saddest part of this story is how easily it could have been prevented. Why in the world did a woman her age still have 80 to 90 percent of her money invested in stocks?

The Perfect Plan

Retirement plans are all different—but they don't have to be complicated. In every case, it's about taking what you have, seeing what your goals are, and working with a knowledgeable specialist to help make sure you pick the right tools to solve those goals.

But one thing is for sure: You're going to want income. If you can plan to have a good income, it solves a lot of problems. It won't make you happy, but when that check comes every month, you sure do feel better about your position in retirement. You can pay for all the things you need, whether it's prescription pills, someone to help you out around the house, or the vacation you want to go on.

Too many people are in a position where their pension and their Social Security aren't enough, and they're tapping into their savings and watching it deplete. They are literally looking at their calendar because they know how many years or how many days, if it keeps on going the way it's going, until they're out of money. When they're that close to running out, it's too late to change things. The ship has sailed, the course has been set. You don't want to wait till it's too late!

Here's how this works for me personally: I have a $500,000 IRA and I'm going to put $250,000 of it into a fixed index annuity and let it start growing with a guaranteed income value down the road in case I choose to turn it on. I don't know that I'm going to need this income, but I'm going to set it aside anyway, just in case. At least that takes the worry out of not having enough income. No one ever complains about having too much income!

The perfect plan is always going to be a customized combination of the tools that are available to you, to get you the most worry-free and stress-free retirement possible. Planning gets you security. It's insurance! It's the safety of knowing that you'll wake up tomorrow morning and nothing will have changed, and even a bad market drop like the one we had in 2008 won't severely affect how you live out the rest of your life.

Think about how you would feel if you had moved a large portion of your accounts into a safety position, and then a market drop happened. You wake up the next day and you're the same. While you may have lost a little of it, you know the bulk of your money is safe—it didn't drop with market conditions. You weren't left waking up after an event that you had no control over, realizing that you lost 20 or 30 or 40 percent of your accounts. At this point in life, you made a smart, common sense decision with your money, choosing to put it into savings vehicles with high security and low risk.

The moral of the story is simple: You don't know what's going to happen, and you don't know how much you're going to need. The only way to prepare for the inevitable twists and turns, dips and crashes, is to come up with the very best plan you can.

CHAPTER 7

FORMER TRUTH #5:
Diversification is the key to safety.

TRUTH: While very important, diversification is not enough to protect you during retirement.

MANY RETIREES AND imminent retirees have the bulk of their money in mutual funds because they want the diversification to lower their risk. While this is certainly true—it *does* lower the risk—it doesn't mean they won't lose money.

Diversification is great! But it's not a secret formula for ultimate safety. You can't just take your money and put it all into mutual funds and say, "Great! I'm very diverse!"

Two Buckets

I want you to think of your retirement money as being in two buckets. First, you have what I call your "live-on" money. This is the money that comes in every month from your Social Security and pensions, including your cash, your CD, your annuities, and whatever else you have. These are your safe accounts. This is the money that is not dependent upon market conditions; it doesn't lose value or change. We call these your "live-on" accounts, because this is where you've put the money that you need to live on, both monthly and for the long term.

Then you've got another bucket called your "leave-on" money. This is the money that may still be invested, and it's going to fluctuate with the market volatility. But this is not money that you need today or tomorrow or at any point in the foreseeable future. If this money drops a little bit, that's okay, because you don't need it right now.

Now picture this: The older you get, the less money you're going to have in your leave-on bucket, because you're moving more and more of your money into your live-on bucket. You want that money in your safety bucket so that it doesn't change based on market conditions.

The way you divide your money between those two buckets has to be age appropriate, and it has to be appropriate for your risk tolerance, too.

You'd be amazed at how many people come in and say, "I'm set, Mark—I'm very diverse." Or, "I'm very conservative—I've invested in more than eight sectors."

Then you take one look at their portfolio and say, "Hey, you may be diverse, but it's all still at risk!"

It's your decision whether or not to put your money at risk, and how *much* money to put at risk. But you've got to go into it with eyes open. You've got to know what you are getting yourself (and your money) into.

There are two types of tools: investment tools and savings tools. Investment tools all have one thing in common: risk. You can make or lose money. "I'm going to buy gold," you say. Great! Buy all you want. Just know that it's an investment tool, which means you can make or lose money, dependent upon market conditions. "I'm going to buy Apple stock," you tell me. Good for you! What does that mean? It means *you can make or lose money.*

The other tools that are available are savings tools. With savings tools, you do not lose or make money based on market conditions. You want to hide your money under your mattress? That's a savings tool—assuming you don't lose the mattress! What's a CD? A savings tool. Fixed annuity? Savings tool. Fixed index annuity? You guessed it: savings tool. Market conditions will not change your principal, i.e., the money that you put in. Market conditions may change what your *growth* will be, but not your principal.

My methodology has always been conservative—after all, I'm trying to *conserve* as much of your retirement money as possible—so I'm going to urge you to take a more conservative approach. As you get older, I strongly suggest you put more of your money in the savings tools, and less in the investment tools. Isn't that just common sense?

The Power of Saving

To show you why, I'd like you to imagine it's 2006. The economy is still going strong and you're a couple years out from retirement. You've got a lot of mutual funds, your accounts are going well, and you are just so happy. Things are going great. Things are going so well that you decide to retire in January of 2008.

Then the big crash comes, and all of your accounts drop—a lot. It's bad, but you're not really too concerned. You've got your Social Security and your pension coming in, and you've got time to let the markets recover. You draw some from your savings to supplement your Social Security and your pension, and you wait.

Fast-forward five or six years. The markets have done well and you've made some money back . . . but you've also been withdrawing this whole time, taking some out each month to fulfill your obligations. All of a sudden, you're looking at the account, going, "Wow, what happened?" You can't rewind the clock to prepare for the big market adjustment, and now you're really having to tighten your belt at a time in your life that you don't want to tighten your belt. You can't take that trip to see the grandkids, because it costs too much.

What could you have done differently? You saved a lot of money. You prepared. The market crash wasn't your fault. So what could you have done? Going into retirement means changing your mindset. Are you willing to risk how your retirement's going to look because you want to leave your money in the market and make as much as you can possibly make? If you want to make the most money, you're going to take on the most risk. You have to think of things like this. If you go into a lower-risk stock or bond, you might lose a chance to make more money, but you also lower your chance of losing your money.

When you go into retirement, you're not trying to make a lot of money. You've done that already—that's what you focused on during the accumulation phase, when you were still climbing the mountain. What you're trying to do now is hold on to your money. You're trying to preserve it.

Will Rogers said, "It's not the return on my money that I'm most interested in; it's the return OF my money."

You have to think about what's really important. Basically, when you start getting close to retirement age, you've either made it or you haven't. You've either got wealth or you don't. If you've got it, it's not going to continue to be that important that you grow it exponentially. It's more important that you don't lose it!

And if you haven't made it, then you sure can't be out there taking big risks, trying to grow wealth fast. If you haven't made it by fifty-five or sixty, you're probably not going to. So let's at least hold on to what we've got! That's just common sense.

But think about how hard it is to act on your common sense. Think about 2006, when markets were doing so well. Think about when they were doing well in 2012 or 2013. It's hard to move your money out of a bullish market and into a place where it won't make the same return. Why would you want to pass on a chance for more money?

Because that's all it is: a chance. And if you're getting ready to retire in four or five years, you don't want to take a chance. You're going into a different phase, and soon you'll be going away from accumulation and going into distribution—so you'd better start moving more and more of your money into safety.

You've got to learn to think differently, to protect what you have.

CHAPTER 8

FORMER TRUTH #6:
A reverse mortgage will solve my income issues.

TRUTH: While reverse mortgages may be fashionable, are you really going to leverage the house you've worked so hard for?

LATELY, A REVERSE mortgage has become very popular. What is it exactly?

Let's say you've got your house paid for, so you go down to the bank. The bank looks at your house and thinks how very nice it is—a beautiful $200,000 colonial with gorgeous hardwoods and a sweeping staircase and four spacious bedrooms that you raised your kids in before they left the nest. The bank says, "I like it," so they agree to pay you $850 a month for as long as you live. When you die, who gets the house? The bank. That's a reverse mortgage.

Who is a reverse mortgage popular for? Many people say, "Retirees."

I say: "The bank!"

Typically, a reverse mortgage is a useful tool for the people who've run out of money. Maybe you don't have enough other income and cash, and you need more money to pay the bills. So the question becomes: Do you move out and sell the house? Or stay there and get a reverse mortgage?

For those of us who have paid off our house and are finally nearing our golden years, it's probably the last thing we want: to mortgage our home. I'm sure I'm not the only one who feels like my house is my castle!

Here's where a reverse mortgage goes bad. Let's say you're living in your home, happy as a clam, and you make the decision to get a reverse mortgage. Then all of a sudden you can't stay there any longer. Maybe you didn't expect to need advanced care but now you do. Because life expectancies continue to grow longer, you've lived well past the age when your father and mother passed, and unfortunately, you do have some health issues that make it necessary to bring in a home healthcare provider. Or maybe your spouse has a condition that requires advanced care. All of these are situations you didn't plan for, because we all hope they will never happen to us.

While your reverse mortgage payment is helping you meet your day-to-day bills, is it really going to be enough to provide for the healthcare you need to have so you can stay at home? Or to get the house remodeled so that it's equipped for a wheelchair and other things you need to stay safe?

If you still owned your home, you could sell it and use the money to provide for your care. But you've leveraged your house for a reverse mortgage, which means you can't sell it. That money is no longer available to you—and now is when you need it most.

The idea of a reverse mortgage is fine if you can stay at your home until you pass away, but that's a very big unknown. If you end up needing more care, the biggest asset you could have sold is completely tied up. If you know for certain you're never going to leave the house, *maybe* it could work—but who knows that? We don't know how long we're going to live or how long we may need long-term care. And what if the neighborhood changes significantly in twenty years and it's no longer a place you need to be?

The Story of Charles and Dorothy

Charles and Dorothy are two of my clients. In their late sixties, Charles and Dorothy had taken out a reverse mortgage. Their home was completely paid for, and their plan was to use the reverse mortgage to provide some extra income for their retirement years. They had a beautiful ranch-style house that they absolutely loved; it was the perfect size and in the ideal location. Their plan was to live out the rest of their days in that home and never move.

But as we've seen, things don't always go according to plan. Fast-forward eleven years to present day: Dorothy is now seventy-eight and suffering from dementia. Because of Dorothy's condition, their beautiful, ranch-style home is no longer a safe environment. Even things that brought them joy eleven years ago—like the sweeping veranda with its breathtaking view—are now hazardous places where Dorothy could fall and hurt herself, or worse.

Staying in their home is no longer the best option for Charles and Dorothy. One option is for them to split up—for Dorothy to go live in a protective, supportive environment while Charles stays in the house—but Charles isn't too keen on that. They've been together for more than fifty years, and he doesn't feel comfortable sending his wife away while he stays in the home they built together. Besides, Dorothy's dementia is not so far advanced that she needs the highest level of care. She may need it in the next few years, but she doesn't need it right now. What she *does* need is more care than Charles can provide in their home.

So what do Charles and Dorothy decide to do? They find a place that offers dementia care but also has independent living. This is nothing like the nursing homes of the olden days—this is a state-of-the-art facility with a full roster of activities and events, as well as the newest equipment and most highly qualified staff. This is a place where Charles can stay active and enjoy a somewhat normal life. He'll have daily social interactions, meet new people, and live independently in his own apartment. He can also be with his wife daily, who is meanwhile benefiting from world-class Alzheimer's care.

In other words: Charles can still enjoy his retirement while Dorothy receives the protective, supportive environment that she needs. As her condition worsens, she won't have to move to another facility; she'll just move up to the next level of care, depending on how the disease proceeds. This will allow Charles and Dorothy to stay together as they have for the last fifty years.

You may be wondering: Where does the reverse mortgage come into this? I'll tell you. That beautiful ranch-style home has a mortgage on it, a mortgage Charles and Dorothy didn't have before. They're still going to try to sell it to fund this next stage of their life, but now they have to pay off their reverse mortgage—a serious burden when they have already had to face so much tumultuous change. They wish they had not taken the reverse mortgage, but they truly thought they were never going to leave! Now eleven years later, the whole situation has changed. In a moment of candor, Charles confessed to me that the reverse mortgage was not the benefit they thought it was going to be.

Charles and Dorothy aren't bad or careless. Far from it—they made the decision that, at the time, seemed like the best decision they could make. But if I'd been advising Charles and Dorothy eleven years ago, I would have urged them to reconsider that reverse mortgage. There were other things they could have done to supplement their income. Charles would feel much better if right now the home was paid for and they could simply sell it, take the money, and use it to help pay for the long-term care that Dorothy needs, both presently and in the future. He is determined to keep this family together; the real tragedy is that the decision they made eleven years ago thinking it would help them in their retirement has actually made their situation more difficult.

Unfortunately, Charles and Dorothy are not an isolated case. I've seen this happen with so many of my clients. Their retirement takes a different shape than they imagined—their health declines or their circumstances change—and suddenly, that reverse mortgage becomes more of a curse than a blessing. I can't tell you how many clients have sat in my office and told me they wished they had investigated other options and set up an alternate income stream rather than accept the bank's offer of a reverse mortgage that looked so attractive five or ten or fifteen years ago.

Yes, some advisors are going to tell you: "Rates are low! Go take a loan on your house!" But personally, I think you should run from that kind of advice. Why put your home at risk as leverage when we just don't know what the future holds?

CHAPTER 9

FORMER TRUTH #7:
It doesn't matter when I turn on my Social Security.

TRUTH: Timing absolutely matters. To make the most of Social Security, you have to time it right.

THIS IS A good one—it's one of the retirement issues people definitely need to look at. It's only natural that you would want to use tools like a Social Security analyzer to figure out how to "turn on" Social Security to the maximum amount. Timing matters—but not in the way people think.

When you look at your Social Security statement, you'll see three numbers. There's an early number, a regular number, and a long number. Here's the deal: You get the most money per month if you wait and take it at your latest date. But that doesn't mean you will get the most *back*.

I've said it before and I'll say it again: We're dealing with all sorts of unknowns when we plan for our retirement. None of us knows how long we're going to live. That's the reality. So saying, "I'm going to wait to turn on my Social Security," may not actually be the best approach.

When are you going to enjoy this money more? When you're sixty-five or eighty-five? Statistically, you are more likely to be in better health in your sixties than in your eighties, so chances are good you'll enjoy it more at sixty-five. Even though it may be a lower amount of money, you're getting it sooner. You've got to think about the time value of money. As we saw in Chapter 2, $1 today is certainly worth more than the same $1 in ten years.

If we take Social Security early, we certainly get to enjoy that money more. Maybe we go on an Alaskan cruise or take the grandkids to Disneyland. And if we *do* pass away early, we certainly got more out because we started taking it early. Yes, we get more money each month if we wait to take it out. And if we don't have an income plan set up to help us with our income needs, we may have to wait. Maybe you'll need to keep working and wait as long as you can to *get* the most you can. But that's typically not going to get us the most money *back* over the course of our lifetime.

This is where the income planning comes in. If you're still working, great. Maybe you're planning to work until you're seventy-five because you love your job. But for most people, turning Social Security on as soon as possible allows them to use that money, enjoy it, and potentially get the most out of it if they pass away early. Even if they live to be one hundred, they still got more enjoyment out of the money than they would have if they'd taken it out later.

It's different for everybody, and Social Security is one of those areas where what is right for you probably isn't right for your neighbors or your best friend. That's why you've got to run the Social Security analyzer software. Do your homework and talk to an expert, so that you don't adopt a "walk down to the office and turn it on" strategy.

Not So Fast

I recently had a married couple come in to meet with me. The husband wanted to keep working but the wife was ready for him to retire. She'd had the hardest job on the planet: a homemaker. I think that's the most noble job there is, to stay home and raise the kids. The most rewarding job, maybe, but certainly the most underpaid!

So the husband wanted to keep working and the wife wanted to retire. She felt like she had more than paid her dues and was ready for some well-deserved vacation time.

"When I get to retirement age," she told me, "I'm going to turn on my Social Security."

"Here's a better idea," I said. "When you get ready to retire, it's better if your husband goes and turns *his* on."

"But he's going to earn too much money!" she

cried. "He'll still be working! He'll have to start paying it back because he makes too much."

"Not so fast," I said. And then I laid out how, once her husband turns *his* on, she'll file for spousal benefits. She'll get more on spousal benefits than her own Social Security. Which means she'll make more than if she had turned *hers* on, because she was primarily a homemaker who worked a lot but not enough (as far as the government is concerned).

Thanks to this bit of wisdom, she'll make hundreds of thousands more over the course of her lifetime.

"That's great!" you say. "How do I do that?"

I'll tell you how: You get a Social Security specialist, pronto. And you work together to plan, plan, plan.

PART III

———

Using Uncommon Sense to Maximize Your Legacy

In Part II, we debunked the seven most common "former truths" of retirement. I hope I haven't scared you with anything I've shared. My goal is not to frighten you, but to compel you—to plan and prepare better, to make the best choices for your retirement. You've climbed a long way and worked hard to get where you are. Now it's time to start thinking about your golden years—about the life you still have in front of you, and the legacy you'll leave behind.

CHAPTER 10

The Sleepability You Deserve

SOME PEOPLE MIGHT tell you that the landscape of retirement is all gloom and doom. "Look at what happened in 2008," they say. "You never know what's going to happen, so you might as well gear up for a bleak future." I agree with the first part but not the second. It's true that we don't know what's going to happen—but there is no reason the future has to be bleak. Armed with the right plan, you'll be able to weather the storms. And it's not enough to simply have a plan; you've got to understand it. A little knowledge can go a long way.

In this chapter, I'm going to tell you the story of a wonderful couple for whom "a little knowledge" changed everything. Their story is not unique; I've seen it all too often in my line of work. For Sam and Jeannie, not being aware of their finances was robbing them of a peaceful, comfortable retirement and keeping them from the life they deserved to live. Luckily, we were able to change the course of their destiny before it was too late.

It all started when two of my longtime clients paid me a visit. I've known Brian and Rebecca for years; they are both in their fifties, and it's been a pleasure to work with them as they get their finances in order to prepare for retirement. But recently, Brian and Rebecca came to me with a question that had nothing to do with their own accounts.

"Can I ask you a favor, Mark?" Brian said. "Would you talk to my parents, Sam and Jeannie? I'm kind of worried about them."

"Sure," I said. "What's up?"

Brian sighed and began to tell me about his parents.

"They sold their house eight years ago and moved into an independent living facility. They're very happy where they are—they've got a real community of friends, and they are always going to dinner parties and game nights. And they're in fantastic shape. My mom does water aerobics every morning and my dad walks three miles a day."

This seemed like a pretty ideal retirement to me.

"What seems to be the problem?" I asked.

"Well, I'm not entirely sure. That's the thing. Lately, when I talk to my mom, she keeps hinting at some financial issues. She's usually pretty vague, but I get the sense they are very worried about money and they're not sure they have enough to stay where they are. They used to love to buy their grandkids gift cards on every birthday and holiday, but recently my mother confided in me that they are worried they're going to run out of money."

"Have you talked to your dad about this?" I asked. Brian chuckled.

"I've tried, but he won't tell me a thing."

I nodded. Sam was ninety years old. Like many people in his generation, he didn't feel comfortable sharing his financials with his son. To tell the truth,

Sam didn't share that information with anybody. He didn't even share it with his wife! Jeannie was in the dark about their finances and always had been. That's why she had been making veiled references to their son—she didn't actually know how concerned she ought to be. All of this is very common; I see it often. Like other men from his generation, Sam kept everything pretty close to the vest.

"Every time I try to talk to my dad," Brian said, "he tells me: 'You take care of yours and I'll take care of mine. I got this.' But I'm worried, Mark, so I'm wondering if you might have better luck."

Brian wanted me to talk to his parents to see if I could get them to open up to me. So I went and met with them privately. As it turns out, Sam and Jeannie were an absolute joy to speak with. They were wonderful people, and the more we talked, the more they began to share.

We sat down at the kitchen table and started going through the Tupperware container that held all their financial information. I asked them if they knew roughly how much money they had, and they did their best to give me numbers. Sam knew it cost them $4,000 a month to live in the independent living facility and that they also paid for health insurance every month. What they *didn't* know was exactly how much they had saved.

"There's a lot we want to do," Sam said. "But we have to live very tight. Each month I take money out of one of my accounts so we can pay all of our bills."

I started by writing everything down so that I could get an idea of how much was going in and out each month. They had a very small amount in their savings and checking accounts, and their only income stream was from two small Social Security checks. Jeannie had never worked, so her check was smaller; together they were getting $1,900 a month in Social Security.

The independent living facility cost them $4,000, and after we added the cost of their phone bill, insurance, and medicine, it came out to $5,500. That's how much Sam and Jeannie needed as a bare minimum to scrape by each month. All it took was some simple math—$5,500 minus $1,900—to see that Sam and Jeannie had a $3,600 deficit. After Social Security they needed a $3,600 spin-down every month, which came out to $43,200 a year.

So I dug a little deeper into the Tupperware container. I found some documents showing that, many years ago, Sam had taken a large amount of money and moved it into several different annuities. Fortunately, they weren't variable annuities—they were fixed index annuities, the same FIAs we have discussed in this book. All those years, Sam had been growing and making money . . . although he didn't know how much.

"I knew we were going to need that money someday," he said. "So I put it away for a rainy day."

The deeper I dug, the more I liked what I saw. When I really started looking at what Sam and Jeannie had in their annuities and other accounts, I realized they had north of $750,000. And these were two people who felt like they were going broke!

So I asked them: In their perfect retirement, what would they do differently?

"Well, the food here is pretty good," Jeannie said. "But we'd like to be able to go out to eat sometimes."

I asked them where they would go.

"We like K&W," Sam piped up, referring to a popular cafeteria-style restaurant around town.

Now, to be honest, I was mystified. This couple had nearly $1 million in their retirement accounts and they were afraid of going out to K&W!

"You can afford to do that," I told them, and showed them how all their various accounts added up.

"But what you have to understand, Mark, is that we don't drive."

"Hire someone to take you!" I said. "You can afford that, too. I don't know how long you are going to live—none of us do. But honestly, I can't envision you spending all this money. It's just not going to happen."

Sam looked thoughtful. "I put that money away for a rainy day."

"Sir," I said, "your rainy day is here. You've been living the last eight years barely getting by. You're so worried about running out of money that you're not spending anything. Your wife feels like she can't buy a new pair of shoes, and you both feel like you can't give your grandchildren the kinds of presents you want to give them. You haven't taken the trips you wanted to take, and you haven't even been going out to eat at the places you enjoy. You are depriving yourselves of all the things you've earned—the stuff that makes your golden years golden."

When I said that, it was like a lightbulb went off in Sam's head. You should have seen the look in his and Jeannie's eyes. They truly didn't know they were okay, and I had just told them they were more than okay: They were golden.

Sam looked at me and said, "You're right!"

"Let me show you something," I went on. "You can take 10 percent out of these annuities whenever you want. Let's put $30,000 or $40,000 or even $50,000 in your savings account right now. That's money to live on. You can go to K&W as often as you like!"

All Sam and Jeannie had done their entire lives

was save and save and save and save. But all the saving in the world is worthless if you don't get to enjoy the fruits of your labors. Galatians 6:7 says that a man reaps what he sows. If you don't reap what you've sowed in your retirement years, when will you?

"You're okay," I told Sam. "To be honest, you're more than okay. You've got nearly a million dollars to get you through the rest of your time on this earth. But you are ninety years old, sir. If you two don't start enjoying that money now, how long are you planning on waiting?"

Sam took his wife's hand and they both smiled at me.

"I guess it's time to start spending some of that money, huh?" he said with a grin. "I just didn't know we were okay!"

If this sounds like a crazy example, it's not. It happens all the time, especially with people in Sam and Jeannie's generation. They have saved so hard and it's all they've ever known. They grew up during the Depression, which shaped their entire worldview. They were taught that money is meant to be saved and never spent; experience taught them that if they broke this cardinal rule, they would suffer. As a result, they end up spending their whole retirement worried about money—even if they have more than enough. They live out decades of retirement paralyzed by fear. It's just not supposed to be that way!

I'll never be able to change decades-long savers into spenders, and that's not what I would advise, anyway. All I want is for my clients to go to bed at night knowing they're okay. I want them to *enjoy* their retirement; to be able to do the things they've always dreamed about doing. If I had met Sam and Jeannie years ago, I would have worked with them to create a plan where they could see exactly how much money they had saved and feel confident in spending it. We would have set up regular income streams, and it would have been important to show them they were clearly okay. That way, they would have been able to enjoy life more and sleep easy at night.

I worked with Sam and Jeannie to close out some of their excess accounts and streamline their income. They took withdrawals from some of their annuities to get their cash savings up. They also got together with their son and laid out a legacy plan. Now Brian and Rebecca feel better, and Sam and Jeannie feel better, too. Even Jeannie feels empowered: If something happens to her husband, she knows what to do.

Fast-forward a few months. Sam and Jeannie are now contracted with a driver who picks them up and takes them wherever they want to go. They leave the independent living facility several times a week to go out and have adventures; they eat out at K&W or go shopping at the mall. Right now, they are planning their dream vacation for next spring. Most importantly: They *feel* different. Brian and Rebecca have thanked me over and over for the difference this has made in their parents' lives.

Here's the moral of the story: Do we really want to have such complicated plans that we don't understand our own finances? Do we want to live in constant fear that we are going to run out of money? No, we don't! Sam and Jeannie only felt certain of one thing: that if they didn't spend money, then maybe they'd be okay. But that did not equate to a life where they could freely enjoy their retirement; instead, they were living in fear and worry. I don't think that is how we are supposed to spend our retirement years.

I see it all too often: couples who work so hard to save, only to retire and worry constantly over whether they have enough to last.

The solution is different for every person. For some it's about turning their money into an income stream that will never run out. Each month they'll be getting enough money to handle their day-to-day expenses and do the things they want to do. For others, it will be a combination of multiple income streams and the knowledge that the bulk of their retirement dollars—their financial security— is safe from market ups and downs, safe from the uncontrollable, unforeseeable events that are all too common in this day and age. What I want for every single one of my clients is for them to go to bed at night knowing that the money they need to live on is going to be okay—and that *they're* going to be okay as a result.

That's what I call sleepability.

What Is Sleepability?

For me, sleepability is going to bed at night knowing that, when you wake up tomorrow, nothing will have changed. The money you've worked so hard for will not be lost due to disaster, greed, or any other issue beyond your control. You will not lose 30 percent of your accounts due to some scandal on Wall Street that you knew nothing about. Your money won't diminish because of a war that broke out in a Third World country, causing international markets to plummet. Your financial future will be insulated from storms and national disasters and riots and calamities and civil strife, simply because you kept your retirement money in a safe place.

People who don't have sleepability can't (and usually don't) sleep easily at night. And for good reason: If they don't have enough of their retirement security in a safe place, they may wake up tomorrow morning to a very different reality. They might awake to the news that 40 percent of their money is simply gone. "What do we do now?" they ask their spouse. "We were going to retire next year." Or maybe they have already retired and are actively spending their money—and it just took a massive nosedive. With that level of risk, I guarantee you those people are sleeping less soundly than the people who have moved their retirement funds to safety.

But if you've got sleepability, you know you're set. Your plan for retirement is flexible; it can change with the times. If you or your spouse gets ill or if one of you is forced to move to an advanced care facility, your plan will adapt. It changes as *you* change. And it's not going to be devastated by events that are completely out of your control.

Then there are the people who sleep just fine at night because they've been lulled into a false sense of security. These are the individuals who favor the ol' ostrich "head in the sand" approach. "We're fine," they think. "What good will it do us to worry?"— when in reality they have not protected their funds. Then a crisis like 2008 happens and they start scrambling to make changes. "Oh, no!" they think. "We need to do something!" So they call me or someone else to help them. I get the busiest when something bad happens, which is the opposite of how it should be. You'd better believe these people have trouble sleeping now!

But by then, something has already happened that changed everything. And when you try to fix it after the fact, there is less to work with. Sure, I do what I can to assist these people, helping them move their remaining funds to security so at least they can rest assured it won't happen again. We divide their retirement savings into the leave-on and live-on buckets, and we do everything in our power to keep that leave-on money safe. Depending on each person's unique set of circumstances, we might decide on a 50/50 split, or 70/30, or 90/10. Maybe we leave in 100 percent. It's a personal decision, but it has to be made. The only question that really matters is: What will it take for them to go to bed at night knowing they're okay?

Whatever your situation may be, it all starts with knowledge. That was the single most important thing in my work with Sam and Jeannie: sharing with them the knowledge that they actually *were* okay. Then we outlined potential pitfalls and discussed the steps we were going to put in place to avoid them. I would do the same for you. The steps would be different, depending on your situation, and they would naturally have to align with your risk tolerance; the tools I recommend will always be age appropriate so that they dovetail nicely with your personal plan. If your plan is to retire down at the beach, then we need to be planning for what it will take to get your cabana and Mai Tais paid for. If your plan is to stay where you are and never leave your home, that's fine—as long as the plan is flexible enough to change when and if life throws you a curveball, like it did for Charles and Dorothy, the couple discussed in Chapter 8.

In this book we've talked about taxes and IRAs and 401(k)s and annuities, which at first glance may seem complex. But I'll tell you a secret: Planning for retirement isn't actually all that difficult. Many of my clients could keep all their money in their savings accounts and they'd be okay. Now, that's not the most appropriate place for their hard-earned money, because it wouldn't earn enough interest to even keep up with inflation. There are much more efficient ways to put their dollars to good use. But the point is, you don't have to get bogged down in a lot of complicated investment tools. You simply have to put that money in the right places.

The good news is: Sleepability is possible for you, too. I've worked in this business for many years, and believe me when I say that it will be okay. I've worked with dozens of retirees, people like Sam and Jeannie, who were living in fear, unable to sleep at night. Then, after we met, we put a structure in place to ensure sleepability. Yes, it involves some planning, but it's not a proposition that's going to take a tremendous amount of time. What it *does* involve is looking at all the options that are out there, writing down what you're trying to accomplish, and putting a plan together. The plan needs to have enough flexibility to change with the times so that you're prepared for all the things that could happen.

Many of the new clients who come to me have been doing the exact same thing with their money that they did ten or twenty years ago—even though they're in a completely different stage of life. Albert Einstein said the definition of insanity was doing the same thing over and over again and expecting different results. I say it's doing the same thing over a long period of time, and expecting the *same* results! If you're still saving and investing money the way you did when you were in your thirties, forties, or fifties, you're headed for disaster. Your life has changed, and the way you save, invest, and spend has to follow suit.

Remember: You're in the distribution phase now, no longer the accumulation phase. You are no longer working for that money; isn't it time to make that money work for you? If you want to rest easy at night, the answer is yes!

CHAPTER 11

Life Insurance: The Gift of Life

When I speak to retirees, I often ask them what their top priorities are. I get a lot of answers, everything from "I don't want to run out of money" to "I want to leave an inheritance to my kids." Almost every man or woman I have ever spoken to says, "I don't want to be a burden to anybody. Not while I'm alive and certainly not afterwards." Different people have different ideas about what's going to happen after they're gone, but nobody wants to burden the loved ones who survive them.

Take Ned and Naomi, a happily married couple who have been my clients for over a decade. They have big plans for retirement—and even bigger plans for the legacy they want to leave behind. They were great savers during the accumulation phase, and they did very well for themselves, creating a sizable estate. As they were both edging into their late eighties, they decided it was time to investigate the best options for how to distribute their estate after they're gone. So we scheduled a time for Ned and Naomi to come into the office for a chat.

Financially, Ned and Naomi were in great shape. They had about 40 percent of their funds invested and they had the rest in CDs and bonds. Although they didn't think they would need income during retirement, they thought they should at least prepare for it. So they put some of that money into an FIA with an income rider that they could exercise if they needed to. Even though they didn't expect to ever turn the income on, it was ready to provide a lifetime income, if needed. And if they had it on and couldn't perform some of the activities of daily living, they could *double their monthly income* for a period of time. They felt good about that, as well they should.

"Here's what we'd really like to do," they told me. "We'd like to leave our children some money, but we also have a charitable organization that we're incredibly passionate about. So we'd like to leave them some money, also. What's a good way for us to do this?"

The three of us talked. What have I been saying throughout this book? *The future isn't certain and we have to prepare for all possible scenarios.* What if Ned and Naomi were wrong? What if they end up needing that money because they live to be 103? Or what if their feelings about the charitable organization changed—say, it fell under new leadership and started misspending funds—but they had already signed their money away and couldn't do anything about it?

There were plenty of tools I could have suggested to Ned and Naomi that would have required them to relinquish control. Perhaps another financial advisor would have urged them to look at some of these options. But my goal is and always has been to protect my clients' savings by keeping the control right where it belongs: with the people who made that money in the first place. So together, the three of us turned our attention to life insurance policies.

Because Ned and Naomi were both still very healthy, we were able to take a portion of their money and leverage it into a very large life insurance policy. Because it was an indexed policy, it allowed them to build cash value and receive a large payment at the time of death that would be paid *tax-free* to their children (any money paid to the charitable organization would already be tax-free). In other words, the policy provided a tax-free death benefit to their children *and* the charitable organization they loved. But we also made it so that they could still access those funds if they chose to. That way, if something went wrong and they needed more money—i.e., Ned became ill and needed expensive care, Naomi outlived her husband by twenty years—they could still go back and get it.

This is a very innovative way to build cash value while simultaneously providing a *transfer of wealth* in a very efficient manner. One thing is certain in this life: We are all going to die. What's neat about Ned and Naomi is that they looked that certainty straight in the eye and planned accordingly. Their plan ensured that, when they pass on, they will also be passing on a large sum of money to the people they care about most. It doesn't matter what the markets do; it's a guaranteed payout with a guaranteed value. Whether Ned and Naomi live two more years or thirty-two, that life insurance policy is going to pay.

If they need more income between now and then, they know where to get it. But if they don't, they have arranged to pass wealth on to their kids and to their beloved charity. They don't have to worry about it anymore: It's a done deal. What if they get unhealthy or experience a change in circumstances? Doesn't matter. They qualified for the policy, they bought it, it's taken care of. And the best part is that their kids have no idea their parents have done this for them. How neat is that? When the time comes for Ned and Naomi to leave this world, what an awesome legacy they will have left for their children—and for an organization doing work they believe in. If you ask me, that's pretty darn cool.

It's About Life

Life insurance is about life. Not just your life, but how your loved ones will live after you're gone. Ned and Naomi changed how their children are going to live after they've passed on. Even better: They did it in a way that will not jeopardize how they live their own lives.

Life insurance is an overlooked portion of planning that could offer you the same opportunity: to prepare for future lives while safeguarding your own. Wealth transfer and asset protection are both hot topics today. People want to learn an official way to maximize the distribution of assets to their spouses, younger generations, and favorite charities. A will or a trust can assign assets to a beneficiary, but these estate-planning tools are designed to preserve wealth, not create it. A life insurance policy, however, can *instantly create wealth*.

For instance, a sixty-five-year-old grandmother can deposit $100,000 into a life insurance policy that passes on *$200,000 or more* to her grandkids. That isn't a typo—she buys a life insurance policy for

$100K and later passes on $200K. That's an instant transfer of wealth! Those grandkids are going to be brokenhearted when their grandmother dies, but what an incredible gift she will have left behind.

I talk a lot about life insurance in my seminars. One of its advantages over an annuity is that income is passed tax-free to the beneficiary. In my opinion, life insurance is one of the safest and most dependable investments for a family—favorable tax treatment and guaranteed returns. It's not a risky investment; it's a savings tool.

Many seniors think they're not healthy enough to purchase life insurance in their golden years. Fortunately, the underwriting allows many people to qualify today who would not have been able to qualify in the past. Often people come up after my seminars to tell me, "I hear what you're saying, Mark—I'd love to get a life insurance policy. I like the idea of passing it on to my kids. I'm just not sure how it would fit into my plan." Let me show you a way that it might.

Using Your Required Minimum Distribution

Take Suzanne, one of my all-time favorite clients. She's a firecracker—over seventy and still sharp as a tack. Suzanne just turned seventy-and-a-half, which normally might not be cause for celebration, but it's an important number. Because she is seventy-and-a-half, she must now start taking the required minimum distribution from her IRA.

The irony is: Suzanne doesn't want to! She's got the income she needs and doesn't want to start dipping into her IRA. But the government says she has to. So what does she do?

First: She comes into my office. Second: Together, we devise a plan.

We're going to take Suzanne's required RMD—money she doesn't need—and use it to fund a life insurance policy for somebody else. Every year, Suzanne will take the required RMD out of her account and *use it as her yearly life insurance payment.* Let's say she has to take $8,000 a year out of her IRA. So we set up a life insurance policy that requires $8,000 a year to be paid on it. Essentially, we are taking the RMD and using it to fund the policy. That eight grand buys a whole lot of life insurance!

Now every time the RMD comes out, it pays the life insurance policy, which will someday pay a tax-free benefit to Suzanne's beneficiaries. Whether Suzanne wants to gift that money to her kids, grandkids, or the non-profit where she's been volunteering for years, it will go to them tax-free. That money is coming *out* of an IRA that's going down, but we're using it to buy something that's going up. When the inevitable happens and feisty Suzanne passes away, the policy will pay out, *plus the balance of the IRA transfers*. How about that? Suzanne is thrilled with this solution—it paves the way for a fantastic wealth transfer to her kids.

Sometimes my clients are not quite sure what to do with unneeded funds. They've got money planned for this and money planned for that, and then suddenly they've got an income stream they just don't know what they're going to do with. Fortunately, that's not a bad problem to have.

If you don't want to spend that money, there are other ways to use it—and paying for a life insurance policy is one excellent way. I love helping my clients set up wealth transfers because we kill several birds with one stone. We can take the assets that the person doesn't need in their lifetime and position them for efficient transfer to the next generation. My clients live more happily, knowing that their offspring will be taken care of, and the lives of the next generation receive a tremendous positive impact as well.

CHAPTER 12

Enjoy Your Money—You've Earned It!

EVERY DAY I work with my clients to find the perfect solution to their retirement needs. They've worked hard for the last thirty or forty years, accumulating wealth and assets, and now they want to enjoy themselves. It's my job to help them preserve their money so that their golden years are just that: golden.

What makes my job interesting is that the "perfect plan" is different for each person. I work closely with my clients to create a plan as unique and individual as they are, specifically tailored to their goals, desires, and risk tolerance. In reality, no plan is "perfect." What matters is that your plan is perfect *for you.*

It's like my wife and I always say: Neither one of us is perfect . . . but we are perfect *for each other*. At the end of the day, that's really all that counts.

There are three traits that all good retirement plans share. We've talked about these over the course of the book, and I'm going to recap them now.

#1. *Your plan should respect your risk tolerance. It should make you feel safe.*

I call this the "eyes wide open" rule. Only you know how much risk you are comfortable with, and your plan should reflect that. And, as you probably know by now, I counsel my retirees to be more risk-averse as they get older, because less risk equates more safety. In the perfect plan, your money is safe because it's in two buckets: the leave-on and the live-on. You know that the money in the leave-on bucket is money you aren't going to touch. You are willing to allow it to go up or down with market conditions. But that doesn't worry you, because you know you have more than enough in your giant live-on bucket, including your cash reserves, fixed index annuities, CDs—whatever you have chosen to grow your money safely without risk. No matter your risk tolerance, there should be enough money in the live-on bucket to know you're golden.

#2. *Your plan should be flexible.*

Your life is going to change. That's inevitable, especially as we age. This is why it's crucial that your plan is flexible, allowing for the ups and downs that are certain to occur. As life's changes come to you, will your plan adapt to meet them?

#3. *Your plan should be simple.*

Your retirement plan has to be simple enough that it's understandable now *and* ten years from now. You don't want to be in a position where you say, "I understand why we did that when I was sixty-five, but now I'm seventy-five and it's no longer clear." You never want your plan to be so complex it takes a CPA to help you understand it. You should be able to grasp the nuts and bolts yourself. In fact, I like to say your plan should be so clear that you could describe it to your five-year-old grandson and he'd more or less understand it.

Greg and Cathy's Perfect Plan

Greg and Cathy are two clients of mine. They first came to see me a few years ago, when they were both still in their late fifties. Together, we devised their perfect plan. Greg and Cathy decided to grow some money in a fixed index annuity while they were both still working. Their goal was to wait until they were seventy to turn on that income. They had plenty of working years left, and a very clear plan for retirement. Greg and Cathy were in great shape.

Fast-forward a few years later to yesterday, when they came to my office to update me on some recent developments. Greg works part-time selling his own line of golf clothes, and Cathy has been working for the last thirty years at a local bakery she absolutely loves. At her age now, Cathy still wants to work! She really enjoys her job, rolling dough every morning and creating a dizzying array of pastries using only the finest local ingredients. The main perk of her part-time bakery job is that Cathy enjoys a nice benefits package that covers her medical and dental care. Until last week, she had every intention of continuing the work and delaying Social Security, because she was still making an income.

Then something changed. The owner of the bakery told his employees that, due to changes in health care, he would no longer provide benefits to anyone working fewer than forty hours a week. And Cathy hadn't worked forty hours a week in a long time—nor did she want to.

All of a sudden, Cathy had lost one of the most important things about her job. Now that she doesn't get medical or dental, she doesn't love working at the bakery quite as much as she used to. So what is she going to do?

This is why Greg and Cathy came to see me. They wanted to know how this would affect the plan they had constructed for their retirement. So we talked for a while, and an hour later, we had the solution. Cathy would go ahead and retire now. She would turn on the income rider from one of their FIAs, which would more than supplement the income she would lose from the bakery. She is still going to delay Social Security so she can get more money later on, because when we ran the numbers, we realized she didn't need a lot more money right now, with Greg still working. Cathy is going to be just fine.

Cathy has also decided that what she *really* wants to do is assist her husband in his part-time business. Greg travels frequently to some of the most beautiful cities in the world to sell his line of golf clothes. So Greg and Cathy have decided that they're going to finally do some traveling together. Cathy will go with Greg, and when he has to work, she can just relax at the club while he takes care of business. One of the major disadvantages of the job at the bakery was the inflexible schedule; Cathy hasn't taken a real vacation in years. Now, she will get to enjoy more quality time with her husband than she has since their honeymoon!

All Greg and Cathy have done is make a decision to adapt the plan. They had no idea the bakery owner was going to change the equation—they assumed Cathy would be working there for several more years, collecting benefits and a paycheck as usual. Life didn't work out that way. But their retirement plan was flexible enough to allow them to make the necessary adjustments. Instead of changing the whole plan, they simply turned on one of their income streams. They were going to turn it on anyway; it makes sense to do it now. Things will continue to function the way Greg and Cathy wanted them to. Nothing changed so much that it will have a dramatic impact on their plan. In fact, you might even say that Greg and Cathy are going to have an even better (and earlier!) retirement than they expected.

A perfect plan should: 1) respect your risk tolerance, 2) be flexible, and 3) be easy to understand. Greg and Cathy's plan met every requirement. They had clearly defined "whens" and "whys" and "how we do it." They had made allowances for changes so that when an unexpected event *did* occur, they weren't taken aback. Their plan had flexibility and sleepability—their money didn't rise and fall at the whim of market realities, tsunamis, and government policy changes. And because they wanted to pass money on, the plan laid out how to do so in a very tax-efficient manner. Greg and Cathy had it all.

The Golden Age of Self-Sufficiency

A retirement plan starts and ends with self-sufficiency. Your goal is to produce self-sufficient income in retirement, and my goal is to help you get there. Our combined goal is to generate the largest possible amount of retirement income that will sustain you for the rest of your life. Pension income, Social Security, FIA income riders, life insurance—the combination is a little different for each of my clients, but the end goal is always the same. None of us wants to worry about having to make ends meet every month. And we certainly don't want to burden our families.

Self-sufficiency is a process that starts well before sixty-five. If you're reading this book in your forties or fifties, that's great. You'll have even more time to plan for your future. If you're already in your sixties or seventies, that's okay, too. I work with people at many different stages of the process, and it is *always* better to face this stuff head-on than to run away from it.

It's definitely a balancing act, aligning what you want with what is possible. While we're balancing future expenses and income, we also have to balance our reality. Sometimes that means adjusting our dreams to the reality of our future circumstances. It's hard work, but ignoring it doesn't make it any easier. You've got to plan for this stuff. You've got to make a decision to *do* something, even if it's as simple as picking up the phone and giving your retirement planner a call. Ignoring your fears and concerns will not lead to a better income. Trust me: It will only make matters worse.

Unless you're fortunate enough to be one of the super-wealthy, you may encounter adverse life events that can devastate your finances. It's an unpleasant reality but true. This is why I work alongside my clients to plan for worst-case scenarios. We all have to take suitable precautions for "the worst that could happen," whatever that may be. That's where sleepability comes in. Your plan should be so secure that you and your spouse sleep better at night, knowing you've got the extra cushion when and if you need it.

What about where you're going to live? You need to have a plan for that, too. Do you want to stay in your house? Are you close to your doctors, your church, and your family? Do you think you'll be better off in a senior retirement community? What kind of community can you afford on your monthly income? It doesn't happen by osmosis; you have to plan for that sort of thing. So let's plan for it. And make no mistake: We're going to plan with our eyes wide open. I can't tell you how many of my clients want to stay in their beautiful home where the master bedroom just happens to be upstairs. In the beginning that's no problem. But ten or twenty years down the line, those stairs start to become an issue. I say: Let's fix that at sixty-five, not seventy-five. Maybe it's as simple as installing an elevator. Or maybe it's going to require a move.

Another thing you must do in order to be self-sufficient is to keep good records. You need a plan that's well laid out and *you must know where it is.* You'd be surprised at how many of my clients can't locate their important paperwork. They know they bought some bonds or invested in that annuity, but they can't find the darned thing. It's crucial that you know where your money is, and that you can easily access the documents to prove it. You want to have multiple copies so that everyone knows where to go when something happens. If not for yourself, do this for your spouse or kids.

You'd be amazed at how few people think of this when they're still young and fit enough to do it. Then they have a bad fall or start suffering from dementia and it's too late. Suddenly, they have left their wife, husband, or kids with a gigantic, heartbreaking mess. Why not clearly lay out what you want them to do? They're already going to be grieving when you pass, so make it as painless for them as you can. "Here's what I got and here's how you get it. Here's what I think you should do."

Key decisions about the end of your life need to be made well in advance. Many people are unable to make sound decisions when they get older because of physical and mental impairments. This is why it must be done early. It's also why you want to see a qualified estate attorney *as soon as possible* to start preparing the necessary documents. In addition to the retirement specialists in our office, we've also got one of Charlotte's top estate and elder law attorneys. That means after clients have met with me, they are able to walk just ten feet and sit down at the desk of my friend and colleague, who then helps them with their estate. It's a very seamless transition, and our clients love it: They like to say we're a one-stop boutique. We handle all their needs under one roof, which makes it very easy for them.

A qualified estate attorney will ask you a number of important questions. Do you want to die in your home or a hospital? Do you want to be buried or cremated? Where do you want your final resting place to be? Do you want to donate your body to science? Have you executed the proper documents to have your spouse or kids make decisions for you at the end of your life?

These are hard questions, but they can't be ignored. A proper retirement plan encompasses every single one. In this book, we've focused more on the financial aspects of retirement, but end-of-life decisions are a huge piece of the puzzle. It's not just you who has to know the answer to these questions; it's your spouse and your children. No one can afford to have his or her head in the sand. Every single person in your family needs to be ready to say, "If this happens, here is what we are going to do."

At the end of the day, can you build a plan that will prepare you for every possible thing that could happen? No. Our real security comes from someplace else. This is merely our financial security. It's about taking the knowledge we have at hand and putting it to good use. Sometimes it can seem overwhelming, but it's not. All you need is a good estate attorney and a good retirement planner. The rest of it is out of our control, so why waste time and energy worrying about it?

At the end of the day, that's exactly what we all must do: prepare the best we can and let go of the rest. Worrying won't do you any good. My happiest clients are the ones who say, "This is where we've ended up, and this is what we've got. So what's next?" What's next is: They're going to enjoy themselves after working so hard. They're going to enjoy their retirement . . . and their money!

That enjoyment can take many forms, and is wonderfully unique for every retiree. Last week I met with a wonderful couple who have been retired for several years. Anna is in her late sixties and Dean is in his early seventies—and they've got a serious case of wanderlust.

"Mark," they told me, "we're going to take some money out of one of our retirement accounts. We've decided to take a trip to the Holy Land."

They certainly weren't asking for permission, not that they would ever need it from me—I'm not that type of advisor. But they did want to know what I thought of the idea.

What did I think of the idea?

"Congratulations!" I said. "I want to go, too! I've always wanted to visit Jerusalem—it's on my bucket list."

My opinion was simple: Use your money while you can! Get every ounce of joy and pleasure out of it while you are still fit and able-bodied enough to do so.

And why not? Dean and Anna have been talking about this trip for decades. Should they wait until they're eighty-five and can't even get off the tour bus, or should they do it when they're still healthy? I told them to go now! Anna and Dean put a plan together years ago, and they clearly understand what they can and cannot do. The whole reason they worked so hard their whole lives was so they could take trips like this one. They can spend that money. They can take the trip of a lifetime with full confidence, knowing they're okay.

You see, Dean and Anna had moved so much of their retirement money to safety, their plan didn't fluctuate with the evening news. They don't have to worry about waking up tomorrow having lost so much of their income that they can't afford this trip. Now they can use their money for what it was intended for in the first place: retirement! And what is retirement if you can't enjoy it? If you're not going to do the things you have always wanted to do? Enjoy your money! You are blessed to have it. Get everything you can out of it while you're still here to enjoy it. We are so blessed to live in this country, what I believe to be the greatest nation in the world. When you compare our lives to those of the millions of people living in pain and poverty, you realize just how rich we are. We are all rich beyond our wildest dreams. A good retirement plan will help you embrace that richness—to enjoy your money for as long as you are blessed to live upon this earth.

The Legacy You Leave Behind

We've talked a lot about uncertainties, the way life changes in ways we never expect. But there is one certainty that every one of us must face eventually: We are all going to die.

I'm not going to talk about what happens after

our bodies breathe their last breath—that's a very different book. But I do want to end with one story about the legacy you leave behind. At the end of the day—and moreover, the end of your life—the perfect retirement plan isn't just for you. It's for the people who love you, the people who live on.

The other day I received a surprise visit from Julia, the grown daughter of my clients Tim and Margie. Margie died years ago, and Tim had just recently passed away. Tim was a kind, gentle man who made sure all his affairs were in order. He had done everything right, keeping his money safe while he was still alive and preserving a good portion of it for his kids and grandkids. He had also involved Julia, his eldest daughter, in every step of the process. If my clients have children who are older adults, I often encourage them to get those children involved in our annual reviews. It can make a huge difference—and for Julia, it did.

"I want to thank you, Mark," Julia said. "The fact that I sat in on all those meetings made Dad's passing so much more manageable."

It was manageable because she understood it. She had made many trips with her father to my office so she could better understand what he wanted, both in his later years and after his death. There was the initial shock of her father dying, and that was very difficult for her. But when it came time to deal with his money, she already knew where everything was, why it was there, and what he wanted her to do with it. When Tim passed away, Julia was prepared, because she had been a part of the plan from the beginning.

"If not for you, I would have been totally over-whelmed," she told me. "My parents used to have accounts all over the place, and I wouldn't have known the tax implications of everything—I don't know what I would have done." She smiled. "Now I see why we did all of this. Knowing what to do and how to do it softened the edges of the loss. Thank you for everything you've done."

This is why I love my job. Helping people like Julia and her parents makes every moment worth it. I'm not just in the business of helping people plan their retirement—I'm helping them enrich their lives, and the lives of their children and grandchildren. Even when your life ends, the lives around you continue—and your decisions continue to affect them.

The truth is, you are facing a future of what-ifs. If you don't have a plan, you'll be completely unprepared for them. But if you've got a plan in place, you will realize why you made the decisions you did when the "what-ifs" happen. Better yet: The people you love will come to understand you gave them a great gift. A lot of the planning you do is for yourself. But you also do it for others—for your spouse, your kids, your grandkids. It's the best gift you can leave them after your passing: the gift of being prepared. That preparation translates into money for your loved ones. They can continue to take income, roll this over, cash this in. Most importantly: They understand, clearly and power-fully, what their options are. And there is no greater gift than knowledge.

I hope you have enjoyed reading this book. If you are interested in continuing the conversation, I invite you to reach out to me by phone or email so we can talk about creating a plan for *your* retirement. Remember: There are no perfect plans. But if you're like other retirees I've helped over the years, there is a perfect plan *for you.*

May your golden years be golden, and filled with what seems to be so uncommon in our world today: loads and loads of common sense.

Best of luck on the journey of a lifetime! And may God bless you.

1-800-689-3935

mark.henry@veritasretirement.com

www.veritasretirement.com

CPSIA information can be obtained at www.ICGtesting.com
Printed in the USA
LVOW10*0801080514

384840LV00003B/5/P